MAY SWIM

Katie Donovan was born in 1962 and spent her childhood on a farm in Co. Wexford. She has lived for most of her adult life in Dalkey, Co. Dublin. Educated at Trinity College Dublin and the University of California at Berkeley, she has worked as a journalist with *The Irish Times*, and has also been a lecturer in Creative Writing, at IADT Dún Laoghaire and NUI Maynooth.

She has published six collections of poetry with Bloodaxe Books: *Watermelon Man* (1993), *Entering the Mare* (1997), *Day of the Dead* (2002), *Rootling: New & Selected Poems* (2010), *Off Duty* (2016) and *May Swim* (2024). *Off Duty* was short-listed for the Irish Times/Poetry Now Prize. In 2017 she received the Lawrence O'Shaughnessy Award for Poetry.

Along with Brendan Kennelly and A. Norman Jeffares, she edited *Ireland's Women: Writings Past and Present* (1994). Also with Brendan Kennelly, she edited *Dublines* (1996), an anthology of writings about Ireland's capital city. She is the author of the pamphlet *Irish Women Writers – Marginalised by Whom?* (1988). She was Writer-in-Residence for her local borough of Dún Laoghaire/Rathdown in 2006-08. In 2019 some of her poems were set to music by the composer Izumi Kimura.

KATIE DONOVAN

MAY SWIM

BLOODAXE BOOKS

ISBN: 978 1 78037 686 8

First published 2024 by
Bloodaxe Books Ltd,
Eastburn,
South Park,
Hexham,
Northumberland NE46 1BS

www.bloodaxebooks.com
For further information about Bloodaxe titles
please visit our website and join our mailing list
or write to the above address for a catalogue.

Supported using public funding by
**ARTS COUNCIL
ENGLAND**

Cover design: Neil Astley & Pamela Robertson-Pearce.

Printed in Great Britain by Bell & Bain Limited, Glasgow, Scotland, on
acid-free paper sourced from mills with FSC chain of custody certification.

In memory of Philip Casey

CONTENTS

I was much too far out all my life
and not waving but drowning.

STEVIE SMITH
'Not Waving But Drowning'

but the sea's secrets diminished on dry land,
darker than they could know or understand

DEREK MAHON
'Calypso'

We live on memory and wonder, on the sense of
connection to each other and to the natural world.
If we allow those things to depart, we are taking
flight from ourselves.

FINTAN O'TOOLE
The Irish Times, 7 January 2023

Deluge

I pass, scarcely noticing the raft:
a leaf, floating in the full bucket
beneath the water butt.
Clinging on, a sailor in the storm:
a soaked bee.
I bring it in, show my daughter,
this striped survivor
of the June showers.
Set on our kitchen table
the bee is offered
mock orange, clover
and buttercup.
First, it dries its fur,
by combing with hind legs.
When the wet is routed
its proboscis delves for nectar.
At last the wings
are energised to whirr,
so we venture out:
a mild night,
getting ready for another downpour.
Undaunted, the bee takes flight.
We smile, and – turning,
find a frilled green moth,
flirting on a tassel like an acrobat,
taking shelter in our light.
At our feet, a snail glides,
smooth and unguent on slick ground,
a woodlouse clinging to its shell:
a miniature rodeo chancer,
catching a free ride
as the flood gathers.

Lost Song

I navigate
drowned forests,
coral gardens,
the backwash of cruise liners;
my swallow drains the tides.
I blow fountains,
my tail divides the sea.

I could last a hundred years
in this playground,
but I fill to starvation
with nets, buckets,
a snagged lump
of plastic cast-offs.

I sing my last song –
an elegy for my family,
for my ocean romps
and mighty leaps.

A human child
finds my drying bulk
flabbing on the shore,
he looks into my eye,
tiny hand petting
my flayed skin.
I groan in my agony.
Poor whale, says the child,
You lost your way.

Polar Switch

(from Dublin to Baffin Island, Canada; video by Paul Nicklen)

Collapsing on a bed of stones
his white pelt loose
as he starves – slowly,
terribly, in a sea of grey –
this polar bear is shared;
goes viral – in his death throes.
He's a warning
to those of us
who shed tears,
as the clip is sent
around our blind alley
of posts and tweets,
as we drink hot coffee
in our tiny freeze –
miles from his thaw.

In a Perfect World

I'd rather my old cherry
with her white earrings
let herself flourish,
instead of drying out
so her sap feeds daughters.

I'd rather holly stopped
eating all the light
in patches of sullen green.

I'd rather the tulip
wasn't gnawed before
she had a chance
to reveal her red.

I'd rather the cleavers
didn't try to climb
over the daffodils.

I'd rather the cat didn't
snatch a blue tit
and eat it.

I'd rather the shed
wasn't a tangle of discards.
I'd rather the children played
in their expensive tree house.

Still – at this full moon,
full Spring, air tart
with promise –
I relish:

the pink flowering currant
and orange-belled berberis;
a bumblebee busy
in the scarlet-starred quince.
The forsythia blazes up,
and the obstreperous wild garlic
offers me flowers
to garnish my lunch.

Arachne's Metamorphosis

(after Ovid, tr. Ted Hughes)

I was ready to wring my own neck,
so as not to suffer the injustice
of a rigged contest.
It was my own fault, I was the challenger,
puffed like a cobra: sure of my gift.
I should have minded my own beeswax:
I, a mortal, rearing on a god.

She wasn't born humble:
she burst out of Jove's head
after he'd gobbled her mother.
So when it came to her picture,
she put herself in the centre
of daddy's charmed circle, sewed hard
to show their awe at her victory
in winning the city.
She garnished her canvas
with punishments, meted out
to those who wouldn't knuckle down.

I have to laugh at her so-called wisdom,
her precious olive branch.
What I got was a box in the head,
when she laid her eyes on my conjuring
of Jove and his shape-changing rapist pals,
busy with their brutal deflowering,
disguised as eagle, bull or swan.
Furious with envy, reeking with poison,
she tore it from my loom,
then forced me from my noose –
my freedom – distorting my body,

so she could boast of mercy;
declare herself mistress of the situation.

Left to crawl in the shadow of leaves,
I lurk in a silk net pumped from my gut.
But, as I abseil from great heights,
spin on my whim – each day a new pattern –
my vision of her curse transmogriphies.

These days she's just a statue: solemn,
helmet stuck on – no spindle, or flashing needle –
even her shield,
carved with Medusa's gorgon grimace,
hangs quite still.

My daughters rule the roost:
many-limbed and eyed, by the time they're born,
their fathers have already been devoured.
Swift weavers all, expert in the hunt,
survivors with their wiles, and much admired.
Mother of such girls, I rarely hanker
for the old tapestries –
frayed and faded in the sun of many days.
Dawn offers fresh vistas in the garden:
intricate circlets, shining with dew,
more satisfying than any crown.
While Minerva languishes – eroded, barren –
with nothing for company but her brittle owls,
I declare the contest finished –
I've moved on.

Wings

A fat bumble,
stunned on stones.
When I lift her clear,
her velvet feet
suction a hold.

For hours she crawls
over the mound of blooms
I lay before her.
Her long black tongue
plunges into nectar heaven
over and over again.

Later, grooming,
her back section levitates
and one wing dislocates –
I fret it has lost its flex
to fly.

After dark I check the altar
of wilted offerings,
every blossom spent.
She's gone,
sleeping off the feast
back in the nest. Wings –
those brittle, improbable fragments –
whirred her home.

Interruption

The cars move forward, endlessly –
it's always rush hour. Strewn
on the road, detritus of the drivers.
And the corpses. Today, a young fox.
He's perfect. I pull over, hoping,
find the body warm.
But as I pick him up – the other drivers
irritated by the interruption – I know
rigor mortis has claimed his fluffy limbs.
The heat is from the sun, shining
all morning on his lifeless form.

The Verge

Violet, bluebell
wallflower,
dandelion, fern –
all rooted here
on a whim –
now gone.

After six bald weeks,
of hard core,
and builder's dust,
the wind carries in
leaf swathes
of ochre and mustard.

Under this coverlet,
small shoots push,
quick to reclaim
their ground –
as though the cutting,
digging, rolling
and packing
was just some ugly
mirage.

Stories

The giant dappled squid
lives deep and dark,
away from the eyes of men.
But stories tell
of a sailor, caught
by a huge tentacle
that swung across his boat.
and clasped him, tight.

So the tensile grip of my desire
swims in her silent haunt.
Do not be surprised
if, one day, her terrible need
forces her into the light,
and, with one long swipe
she takes you, whole.

Invasive

They quiver: two sycamores
shaken to their inmost rings.

Huge, statuesque, they grew
from a twin leaf shoot,
found their grip and soared.

Today a man conducts
a butchering,
to sabotage their symmetry,
the strength they've built,
their mighty branches,
impervious to wind.

A ghost of their future
flits like a lone crow on the wing.
Perhaps now is when they'll begin
to relinquish their hold,
cease their helicopter bounty,
their ankle-deep leaf fall.

After the saw stops,
and the raw discs are chipped,
dust falls like ash
across the January grass.

By May, the trees
have dressed their winter wounds
with clusters of mint green leaves,
lifting a canopy
for squirrels and birds,
dangling flower tassels
for droning bees;

not in full sail like before,
thanks to the small man's
attempt at mastery –

but still magnificent;
and still filtering
the air he breathes.

Foxed

A thief, a killer, a miscreant.
Ignored, despised, driven out.

I

He waits in the garden,
shivering in the evening chill.
Inside, we are full-bellied
warm and well.
His fluffy ears and smart black socks
look fine, but his flanks are bald,
his tail a dangling rope.
His skin is on fire
with pestilent mites.
Snap! go his hungry teeth
scratching himself.
Three weeks now
he's been turning up for this:
a dish of meat
laced with healing drops.
So far, there's been no change.

II

He wanted a lifeline
that day he crept close
to show me his ruined coat.
He'd lost everything:
heat, rest, comfort,
the energy to scavenge –
even fear. The upshot of mange
is slow starvation.

I've had enough
of watching death win:
I took the challenge.
I reeled him in.

III

He hunches, bone thin,
back legs tender
and limping.
The bands of fur
around his eyes
are ringed
with crusted tracks,
they show the impact
of the disease, its deep
unravelling.
The ginger cat stalks him,
but he's not tuned for play.
He shies, accustomed
to being moved along.

IV

The birds are busy
flitting and darting,
enjoying the long day,
boasting of nests.
Under their feeder
fox slinks, hoping
for dropped nuts.
What I give him
is never enough.
While they sleep
in feathered bunches,

fox finds the outdoor larder
I've forgotten to close
in the back.
He drags out
a pack of biscuits,
scoffs the pink slabs
and gulps down the paper.
One day he found my glove
and ate the leather finger.

V

He sets aside
the raw bone he will cache
to eat later,
in the lean hours.
He licks out the dish
then lifts the bone
firmly in his jaw,
trotting off with purpose.
He's back at twilight,
as the cold sets in
wanting more –
I see the pus-filled lump
on his tail; I assemble
salmon scraps
laced with Echinacea.
I've a lot riding on this fox.
I'd better not fail.

VI

He sits waiting, ears cocked,
circling when I emerge,
bowl in hand, redolent

of the butcher's floor:
off-cuts I have begged
on his behalf.
After eating, he lingers,
curling beside
his feline double:
a ginger pair
toasting in the sun.

VII

He likes stale cake,
his ears lie flat
and his jaw works blissfully,
his whole body
focussed on it,
like an arrow.
I find a patch
of pressed grass
where he lay,
long dry stalks
make a fine summer bed.

VIII

By August,
his pelt has regrown,
his tail sports of dot of white
at the tip. His golden eyes
survey the garden.
Next door a drill grinds.
The rain slaps down.
He holds his ground
and waits. This
is his place.

IX

Fox sees the front door open:
it's quiet, and the waft of food
tempts him. He slips in.
The kitchen door is closed
so he slinks upstairs.
The rabbit thumps
her back foot on the cage floor:
alarm. The two lady cats –
whose domain this is –
hiss and fluff their tails.
Hearing the outcry,
I huff past the feline flurry
to my bedroom, where
I find fox, cowering
beside the bookcase:
cornered, but looking oddly
at home. I chase him back down
to the garden, where he waits
for the mistress of larder
to provide. After he leaves,
I soothe the rabbit,
the cats, my children.
We even put the chain on.
We've had burglars before.
We've lost a rabbit too,
years ago, to one of his brethren.
But really, he has taken nothing,
just upended our assumption
about what belongs outside,
and what comes in.

X

Even without the flash
of his russet coat,
I leave a full dish,
in good faith, until
I see the cats at it.
They guzzle
the smelly fare
they'd never normally
touch – just
to deprive their rival
of his portion.
It's five days now
and all of us
are flummoxed:
this fox was one of us.

POSTSCRIPT

I don't check for him,
I don't peek or tune in
to the silent garden,
I don't linger
over cheap meat
in the shop.
I never wonder
if he's alive. I never
dream of him,
his coat, that I revived;
his wild eyes.

Midsummer Rescue

Golden sacs of pollen
heavy on her back legs,
the bee has lost wing power.
She feeds eagerly,
crawling on blue flower studs
of green alkanet.

Rested and satiated
she makes a break for it,
taking off from my hand
like a tamed bird of prey.

Her flight is brief –
she falls onto the crisp mesh
of last year's montbretia.
I place her on a dish
with blossoms and a sup
of sugar water.

Night comes, and with it
an onslaught of slugs
drawn to her bed.
She clings to the edge,
too weak to leave.

I bring her in,
pierce a box with holes
for air. When she's settled
with water and soft paper,
her anxious buzz dies down.

The bee I found earlier
on the grass verge,

lies still – brittle
and finally dead.
It took her twelve hours
to surrender. I dropped sugar water
on her tongue, and laid
her heaving form
on a hot water bottle
to keep her warm.

It's all go at the bee hospital:
every day since April
my daughter and I
have tended the casualties.

Now midsummer, bodies –
like furry buttons –
litter the pavement:
squashed by feet,
drowned by rain,
devoured by parasites,
poisoned by sprays.

Survivors work overtime,
nimble and buoyant,
gathering nectar
as each flower opens –
dog-rose, bramble,
the yellow cups of poppy.

In the morning,
our bee in the box
with her golden sacs
is awake, and ready to go.

I release her:
a striped scrap of fluff,

quivering
as her wings lift her free.
She flies straight up,
over the house –
into the sun.

Détente

Battling to control
the bindweed, bramble,
valerian tangle,
forays of ivy and nettle
I slash, tug,
dig, unravel
but still
I'm losing ground.

Better to accept
peace offerings:
bindweed's blossoms
of creamy silk,
where a tired bee
crawls in to shelter
and stays to drowse;
nettle's gift
of fluttering, sun drunk
red admirals.

Ivy's dark fruit
draws pigeons;
its glossy leaves
are camouflage
for nests.
At summer's end
brambles swell
with sweet-ink berries
to tempt our tongues.

The valerian,
working its roots
into the stone wall,

waves defiant flags
of white, red, pink,
reminding me
it's possible
to thrive
on almost no ground
at all.

Honeycomb

The digging was easy and although they often broke off to feed or merely to sit in the sun, before mid-day Hazel was out of sight and tunnelling between the tree roots...

RICHARD ADAMS, *Watership Down*

I'd seek her
in the back garden –
a small walled wilderness
of wild garlic and gnarled quince.

Her nose would lift,
sampling the scent
of sweet pear, carrot,
or lettuce – her favourite.

After nibbling her prize,
she'd lick her paws
to wash her face,
then open her mouth
in a dainty yawn.

I'd gaze at the length
of her chocolate ears,
the ruff of soft nesting fur
beneath her chin.

At twilight it took three of us
to corral and bring her in
to the safety
of her straw-filled cage.

She wanted to remain
where her busy claws

could express her gift,
throwing up clouts of soil
snuffling down
into the dark joy of it.

She'd stretch
in the smooth runway
of a finished burrow,
perhaps dreaming
of the kits she never bore,
or relaxing
in the pride of her craft.

That's where she lies now,
lapped in the earth
her work has shaped.

I still forget, go out,
bearing cauliflower leaves,
or apple peel –
stand alone
in the garden,
my wilting gifts
mere compost.

My Fluffy Valentine

Plush plump
dark-padded flirt,
slinking my shins,
stalking on the stairs.

White chin and whiskers,
lighten his camouflage,
green eyes glint
as he purrs:
bed-time.

The whole tabby roll of him
surrenders to heat,
his silky, ochre belly
groomed toasty clean,
his marbled tail
wrapped and curled up neat.

He sighs, satisfied
to be master
of my sleep.

Recycling

I sluice through puddles
nursing my hunger
for succulent salmon,
tender tuna, wrapped
in sliced seaweed,
plumped with rice,
heady with mustard
and tongues of ginger.

Prawn, eel, crab;
deliciously dipped
in dark soy –
a tastebud treat
to savour.

But what am I really
putting into my mouth?
For my long,
pulsating digestive tract
to assimilate?

Every morsel
the sea creatures ingest
I will swallow.
Necklaces
of tiny plastic beads
flow from their flesh
to mine –
the return
of my bubble-wrapped,
styrofoam-packed,
ziplock life.

Murder

Hoodies or glossy jackdaws
lunge and nip at the feeder;
rummage in the leaf litter,
hoppity jig on the grass,
dandy in their pantaloons.

In apple time they thieve fruit
and roll it across the roof,
the orbed feast a tough prospect
when you've only got a beak.

As the light fails, they hunch
on spindly branches
in companionable groups.
They sway as the wind lifts
their feathers; exchange
'ark's and *'crrk's*
from a day of gliding, foraging
and keeping watch.

One takes a figary
and leads a scatter
of black swirling bodies
to the night tree to roost.
Later I'll hear a croak –
from an inquisitive look out –
one eye open
while the others doze,
bunched together,
talons gripping perches,
sharing safety, heat, rest.

Shelter

A warm wet night,
and clumped leaves
on the path
rustle with frogs:
a mottled, muscular male;
and his smaller mate.

She is dotted
with pale splodges –
I learn later it's herpes:
they live with it, as we do.

He will dig down,
into the mud of the pond floor,
when the weather turns.
She will bury
her translucent body
under rotting autumn debris.

The last one I find is tiny:
moss-coloured,
not one bit pleased
to be discovered. Gone
next day, when I return
to spy again.

They seek shelter
in this wild place
that still offers
a space for fox, squirrel,
badger, hedgehog.

It's the opposite
of tended or dainty,
yet roses and lilac thrive.
I like a tangle, a few thorns.
Corners filling up
with unexpected lives.

Needle

The only kitten in the tabby litter
to emerge full ginger – quixotic, finicky –
her round eyes fixed on me.

Now when I offer morsels of meat
she stalls – barely licks warm gravy.
Refuses milk. Yet is clearly hungry.

She purrs and arches as I approach,
comb in hand; pushes her head
against my wrist. Then wilts.

In spite of what's prescribed,
the tumour bloats, shrinking her
from lithe dancer to hunched husk.

She shivers in her soft coat –
cream and apricot, tigerly striped.
The breath burbles in her throat.

The day comes when I must submit.
I take her to the arid clinic
and the final, hated needle.

Nothing is as empty as the house
without her. Her light step. Her eager cry;
her dryad form in its autumn gold.

The Three Who Were Lost

I was the first who stayed alive.
Like some painted over canvas:
the consolation prize.
Then, at last,
a boy, big and bonny
and full of smiles.

He and I carry on
into middle age,
while she still dreams
of the three who were lost.
She has travelled, searched;
adopted others
to assuage her need.

I had my two with ease.
None of her terror,
wondering *can they breathe?*

She never said a word –
except once, when I complained
my son could not latch on,
drew blood
as he gummed fiercely
at my breast.

Be grateful for what you have,
she told me.
Her voice was very hard.

Baby Feet

Their little feet –
chubby plump,
unable to take weight –
shod in sky-blue slippers,
appliqued in moon and stars.
Now they run
in worn out, scuffed boots,
mucky and soon too small.
The blue slippers
remain pristine –
they grew up so fast –
hardly used at all.

Home to Vote

(Dublin, 25 May 2018)

They burst through customs,
a river of Repealers,
returning to swing
the referendum;

whooping, twirling, laughing,
just when the last banner
has been hung,
the last leaflet delivered.

'We're home now,' they say,
fresh off the ferry, the plane:
'Let's do this.
We're here to win.'

Fleets of cars take them
to the polling stations,
motoring through
Friday traffic, all the way
to Cork, Galway, Clare.

They share selfies,
revel in pampering
from delighted parents:
the pubs are full
and it isn't Christmas.

Back from Vancouver,
New York, Dubai,
they stay up all night,
and when the vote is sure,
they flood the streets,

they take the Castle,
dancing farewell
to secret crossings;
to danger, to shame.

Let's Go
(i.m. Ashling Murphy)

Shall we run?
Let's run away
so it's never hurt –

the delicate cradle
of the pelvis,
its secret fruit.

Let's run
like the deer in the mountains,
with the snow
and the cold night air

So light
So free.

Two Women, One Grave

Now, at last,
she wants to see his grave.

This is our first time
meeting: she turns out
to be small, straight-nosed,
determined –
oddly familiar.

It was she who ended it,
their long engagement;
moved on, to a better job,
a certainty she needed –
more than he had to give.

As I puppet my way
through the narrative
of his illness, she grows still.
It is a long drive to the grave,
and I wait
while she has her tears.

I'd like to blame her
for something.
She'd like to pour balm on me.
She thinks quietly –
I imagine –
of her lucky escape.
I think of his misery.

But we are alive now,
and he has been gone
for seven years.

So I drive more hours
and we speak of our children,
as women do:
we women,
who live
long enough.

The Diggers

The trampoline
their father rigged
for our children's fun
must be dismantled
for the clearing.
Diggers are coming
to disinter our septic tank.
A brand new one,
with a filter,
and all the mod cons,
will be sunk in the garden,
between clumps of chalky soil
and hunks of granite.

I roll away the frame –
like a ferris wheel upended –
and hook it on the arm
of the elephantine sycamore.
A disc of ivy trembles
as a mottled frog loses cover.

The dish where the robin likes to bathe
must be moved, all the pots
ranked elsewhere, out of the way.
The one old rose, barricaded –
its root too deep to lift –
daffodil bulbs dug up and saved.

The children are so tall. They've outgrown
the blue slide that went to the dump
last summer. The basketball hoop
is rusted through. The boy
has a husky voice, and the girl

asked me yesterday if I could explain
this word she heard at school: *porn*.

I wonder how the daisies will feel,
torn and scattered;
how the earthworms will survive,
ripped out of their home.
Change: I scold myself
for cowardice:
I've seen enough real graves.
I know the difference.

After the carnage,
I'll reinstate
the trampoline –
remember
how the screws fit,
and the safety net sits;

I'll bury the bulbs
for the rebound.

Beaming

It's twenty years
since I first watched him –
dextrous and handsome
in his tux – play cello
along with plangent brass;
oboe; the drum roll
of percussion;
innocent of what was to come.
Now I sit with our children,
in the audience again.
My boy: tall; fourteen,
turns to share a smile.
My girl, with her sea-green gaze
and petal cheeks, swims deep
in the swell of sound
and the dance of coloured light.
No high classical here:
we are tuned
to the signature notes
of Spock, Yoda and McFly:
the transports of Hollywood Sci-Fi.
The players sport costumes,
festive as Solo, Vader, Rey.
In the shelter of the music,
I grieve,
for what was quenched
in the onslaught of disease,
marching
like the stormtroopers of doom.
When the last crescendo dims,
and the musicians take a bow,
we float out of the hall.

Flanked by two golden,
chattering heads,
I am proud: they flourish
into adulthood;
fingers alight
with their father's gift.
I beam as we walk
along familiar streets,
where their parents
once took
a post-concert stroll,
shared a first kiss.

Snowman

After the blizzard,
the road is cleared;
bread and milk
are finally delivered.

The retreat of ice
leaves slush;
drip of melt
from the eaves.
Birds sing of their survival
through the freeze.

Ten years ago
a different storm
blew in – froze us,
brought him to the hospice,
buried Christmas.
When it left
his breath went with it.

Our snowman's head shrinks,
loosening his stone teeth.
I begin to fear this thaw.
What will be uncovered
once the blanket is lifted?

Nothing is ever finished.

Archaeology

In the dank air
of November,
I take a figary
to go harvesting.

Time to repot
the grape hyacinth
so it's ready for spring.

I squat with my trowel
reaching in
for the rich loam
at the bottom
of the compost bin.

Wondering how long
the apple and potato peel
have been settling,
I glimpse a flash
of silver and sky blue,
dig out a worn spoon.

I recall him
swooping to feed
small gooey mouths
opening like birds
until they learned
to clutch the handle.

Teenagers now
they don't recall
much of their father,
and when I brandish,

in triumph,
this souvenir
of high chair meals
shared together,
they shrug.

I return to the garden,
and my laden bucket,
spreading the compost,
observed by hopeful robins.

The spoon sits alone
on the empty table;
a small, clean memory
sprung from the midden.

Portrait of the Mother as a Clay Teapot

I drive at dawn to Irish College
for the Sunday visit
my son's permitted.

Connemara vistas fly by,
but I'm primed
for the moment I spot
his much missed face,
squeeze him tight.

He tells me survival here
comes from strumming guitar;
banter with friends,
mining humour from this ordeal.

My urban, godless child
cannot speak with ease
this remote ancestral tongue;
is irked when it's assumed
he'll go to Mass.

After we've lingered
for hours in Clifden
I leave him
for my long drive back to Dublin.
Ten more days until he's home.

Later, he sends a text:
at the compulsory *ceilí* in the stuffy hall,
he committed the fateful crime
of surrendering to tears:
The most embarrassing moment of my life.

I had been thinking it was worth
cramped hours at the wheel,
to deliver maternal cosseting,
but I'm no rescuer –
just a squat,
clay-footed teapot
spouting steam.

Undertow

Sea water swirls towards us,
froths like an eager dog
then retreats, pebbles clicking
with the rolling drag.
This is my elixir, I'm excited
to have lured you here.
Your poor limp body.
Your sleepy feet.
Will the water waken you?
Lick you back to shape?
The current hurls a big wave
crashing at us, the spray
peppers your shins.
You've had enough.
You hunch, drying your toes
with an attention
that gives me hope, perhaps
your push to clean the sand
so thoroughly is the sign I need?

Later you lie on the sofa,
iPad in hand. Hunched, silent.
I must draw back,
restrain my tide of expectations,
refrain from tugging you
to places that don't suit.
I seethe in my impotence.
Dream of my own swim,
slipping past the breakers
to find my rhythm.
Ignition.

First Aid

Will I break her ribs?
Snap her clavicle?
I press and count:
One, two, three, four,
a burn kindling
in my braced legs.
My daughter holds the phone
as the emergency lady
guides us,
as we take it in turn
to dissuade
my mother's heart
from quitting.

It's not the same
as learning First Aid,
practising on a doll.
This my girl's
grandmother, sprawled
on the floor – loud,
brash, stubborn as hell –
now, just a shell.

At last, the First Responder
finds us, takes over;
the ambulance team
fires up a defibrillator;
she's stretchered
down our narrow stairs,
and sirened to the ICU.

We are left
in the shaking house.

It's a Friday morning,
she had just
eaten scrambled egg,
in bed, said she felt
a little better,
ready to get up.
Next, we heard the crash.

Picnic in the ICU

Do you remember
my brother asks
that wild party?
The one that turned
from orgy to burglary?
She gives a start
and we laugh,
fooling ourselves
that – through the sedation,
ventilation, pace-maker –
she can hear us;
is impatient
to have her say,
about how hard it was
not to scold her son
when his friends' shenanigans
took over the house.

We know she'd like
to join in,
as we reminisce
and snack on cheese straws
dipped in hummus.
But actually, she is sinking
so deep in the caverns
of the underworld,
that she has forgotten us,
her delicate, intricate
necklacing neurons
misfiring:
aftershocks
from her damaged heart
that will not last the night.

The Dragon-printed Robe

In the storage depot
I pace long corridors.
The lights, if I'm immobile,
go out, leave me in a darkness
of closed doors, units full
of shrink-wrapped heirlooms,
waiting for a trolley
to lift them home.

I unlock number 229
where the objects of her life
are piled, boxes brimming
with books, artwork,
mirrors, winter boots;
a yellow table; her knitting wool.

When will she be back? they ask.
We came to furnish her new house

Never, I reply, dodging
as a carpet lands on my head,
and I dislodge teetering shelves.
Slicing Sellotape, I cut myself,
resort to ripping cardboard
with bare hands.

I'm here to sort for charity,
I declare, as I disinter
a horde of buttons;
familiar peach perfume –
failing to quell nostalgia
as I uncover
a mint striped jug; red salad bowl;

the dragon-printed robe
I brought her years ago,
all the way from Tokyo

Walk On By

(for Jamie)

My aunt brought the song
to our lonely house,
it lived on a thin disc
that came alive in a box.
Dionne's voice
was actually her,
I was convinced, and so
after she left us
to return to London,
I would stand at the gramophone
calling her name
as the damp days unspooled
in a dull parade.

It would be months
before she'd come to Wexford again,
and my mother's face would change.
Together they'd fill our dingy kitchen
with laughter, and the glossy tossing
of dark hair. I'd hide my eyes
and hear the tinkle of a bell
to herald the fairy's gift –
a surprise they'd concoct
from oddments in hand's reach.

Now she's alone: my mother
has walked on. Just an echo left
of the fun they had, the furious fights.
The tie that would never unknot.

Signs

After twenty years
the amaryllis,
like some geriatric triffid,
is pushing out a swan-necked
neon green bud.
Is it a sign?

My mother is still dead.
She's the one who gave me
the obstinate plant.
My daughter is still sick.
She's the one
on the brink of her life –
a bud in her own right,
refusing to flower.

I'm seeking
a hopeful metaphor,
but in spite of the newly galvanised
ambitious amaryllis,
and the sun it's stretching for –
nothing fits.

Death and Taxes

Every year as the leaves turn
and the berries ripen,
I face the tally:
earnings, receipts
what I can claim in 'relief'.

This year the record
sticks in October,
my last swim,
my daughter starting college.
My mother's needs
obtruding after her years
living abroad.

I never reckoned
that her return
would spiral
into doctors and hospital,
draining her strength,
until she was propped
in bed, like a river
dried and choked
from drought, her life
shriven to suitcases,
her cat cowering
in our unfamiliar house,
her fears shared
only with her sister.

With me she gathered
her thinning dignity,
saying I had saved her,
only to collapse and turn blue
before I could.

Midlife Crisis

I can't help envying
my new automatic car,
with her pearlescent gleam.
My skin is wrinkly, my hair thin,
my teeth yellowing.

When I drove our old van
I didn't worry
when it got scratched (again)
on our stony lane, or when
three pairs of soccer boots tramped in.
Just that unsolvable issue
with the brakes – forced me
to move on.

I should be happy –
after years of jalopies,
she's the car of my dreams –
a hybrid saloon.
Sleek, slanty-eyed:
a show-room siren.
But I'm a bit past it
to learn her tricks,
and my back complains
when I twist
and slide inelegantly in.
No clutch or hand-brake,
just beeps
that addle me when I reverse,
and, as for my left leg –
it might as well not exist.

But she runs like a whisper,
light and lean,
and she's clean.
She's the future –
I must take the challenge –
I will grow to love her,
and I will outlast her.

Salad Days

I'm sorry,
you can't be a poet any more –
you aren't young or sexy now;
or even a beautiful person
whom everyone online adores.
You haven't had a lover in years
and your children are teenagers.
You look all right – but not in photos –
and worst of all
you're so peggable as a mum.
That's you in the supermarket, right?
hovering over spinach
dreaming up a nice school lunch?
You should be slumped
over espresso in some NYC lookalike café,
or drinking wine as you pen
another lyric to heartache.
Stop thinking about feeding the birds
and paying the heating bill.
Don't eat any more chocolate,
and, as for cheering your son on
while he plays soccer –
have you totally lost it?
If you could have just frozen yourself
circa 1995, when you wrote that one poem –
you know, that ended up
by freakish chance in *the* anthology? –
you might have managed
to remain a viable presence
on the poetry scene. But now,
well, truth to say (unless you're prepared
to give a reading for a fund-raiser –
would you be? for free?)
you're just a has-been.

Spain

All night the sea shushes
and I cradle the ache –
it kindles in my right thumb,
the shoulder a bowl of pain.
How could I be the one
to suffer this, to succumb?
I who invite others
to lay down
their tears, their torsions.
Yet this last night
of my beach sojourn
of lolling and basking
with my children
the ache takes hold.
I wake to the struggle
of the rental car:
once more my brain
must achieve the swap
of left- to right-hand drive.
I haul loaded cases
full of dirty clothes,
negotiate unknown roads
with stark rock terraces
and steep valleys.
In the back the children –
guessing mother
is sliced thin –
suspend their squabbling;
my girl navigates,
my boy sings of home.
Like the crusts
that contain the loaf
my hands stay constant
at the helm.

This Singular Horse

(20,000 year old art in Tito Bustillo Cave, Asturias, Spain)

Women made most of the oldest known cave art paintings
– *National Geographic*, October 2013

She left the light
for the deeps inside the mountain,
carrying black and violet dyes,
crushed from whatever
she could lay her hands on.

In her mind, the horse burned,
urging her through serried pillars,
medusa formations of weeping stone.
She must have had a torch,
a ladder to reach the ceiling,
more than one companion.

As I retrace her journey
through freezing caverns,
I wonder about her children:
as she painted,
did she tell them stories,
so they wouldn't stray?

They'd have been riveted
by tales of equine derring-do,
and stolid oxen:
the path of narrative
lighting the vaults
of their growing craniums.

A listening child
might not recall
this singular horse
until years later:
a chance ignition
revealing the picture
in all its buried, lonely splendour:

nostrils trembling,
ready to breathe again.

Berkeley

(16 June 2015)

Crack of rotten wood,
the balcony tips and swings,
hands grasp – some
not fast enough, some
too slippery –
plummeting, smashing bones
to smithereens.

Mothers fly across the world,
hoping to hold them again,
to hear them breathing,
those babies who suddenly
grew up, now stretched
in stiff white hospital beds.

Eucalyptus and coffee,
peaches and sushi,
maverick conversations
fit for branching neurons –
Berkeley, where I grew
for two full years,
out of my small Irish plot,
into a nourishing garden:

now you are a graveyard,
a valley of fallen stars.

Olive Trees, Provence

(i.m. Phoebe Donovan)

I

Silver-green leaves
shimmy
in the warm breeze;
tickle the blue sky.

I think of her, here,
fifty years ago,
a cigarette dangling,
easel planted.

II

From my balcony,
the angle changes;
the sea sparkles
and the air is bleached.

Oleanders in pink and white
mirror bathers
with blow up rings,
heading for the beach.

A train spools past,
pigeons make their soft
hollow call;
brassy cicadas
sing to the heat.

A butterfly –
like a scrap of lace –
soars above shadows
as the sun devours
the afternoon.

Underneath the olive trees,
a young man flips
over and back
on the dappled grass:
somersault; arabesque.

Rome Project

She writes her project
on Roman boys,
because her teacher told her
the girls didn't have
much of a life;
were often left as babies
out on the street
to die.
Until a law was passed
making it illegal.
At least they did that
she said.

Shapeshifting

(Armação de Pêra, Portugal)

Water and sky
merge to soft indigo
as we slip, she and I
into curving wavelets
melting on the shore.

A small bar
casts a sprinkle of light
on two children
skipping in the cool sand –
while a lone swimmer
strikes further out.

We wade and float,
held by velvet eddies;
my daughter
in her pink bikini,
beautiful, unaware, fifteen.

After, we scamper
to our towels,
wrap and linger;
stroll – sticky with salt –
past the whisk of grasshoppers,
blurt of frogs.

We throw scraps
from our fish dinner
to the wild cat
and her kittens,
hiding in the dunes.

When I hear
the loud voices,
of drunk boys singing,
I quicken in concern –
once, I was prey.

Our mirrored feet
follow mosaic tiles
into the darkness
into what's left of our days.

May Swim, White Rock, 2020

During the Covid-19 pandemic, the Irish government
permitted citizens to take exercise only within a 2 km
radius of their home.

I wade in,
my hands wringing
from the pain
of the water's
freezing touch, its greed
to suck the warmth
from my toasted skin.

After immersion,
every cell tingles:
glowing and replete.
I peel off wet togs
and dress –
the clench of fear
released.

I'm a sea pink
blooming in the rocks.

Salvage

(May 2020)

Spring sky,
white cat,
bluebells:

cobalt, silver,
and delicate,
frilled pinks.

They rise
through nettle,
bramble,
wild garlic.

The cat prances;
the bluebells offer
their silent music.

Once I picked
an armful
from the woods:
I was six.

Now I see
a snapped stem,
and reach to save it.
I place the orphan
in water,
on the windowsill.

Drink this, I say –
and live.

Marking Time, Dalkey
(May 2020)

Our morning swells
with the sonority of bees –
bumbles, in their fluffy coats,
hover over the rosemary
and wild garlic;
sip from the pink cups
of lungwort.

Afternoon, and a kayak
pulls in at the island,
where distant goats roam;
we squint in the sun,
spotting a seal lift
his salty, whiskered head
from the rippling water.

Later, in the quarry,
where we take an evening stroll;
a lone wren fills
the gorse-studded hollow
with resounding song.

The setting sun
warm on her back,
a fox creeps
along secret paths;
reaching the tall grass,
she rests by the cowslips,
under our apple tree.

Catching Flies

A fly wanders in
unwary of the trap.
But when I try to help it out
of my stuffy house
it uses every ruse
to elude my cup.
As a fly-rescuer
I have patience and focus
but it can't tell
I'm not a threat.

Some retreat so far from me
that by accident they find
the right window crack
to buzz back to the sky.
Others lose momentum
and are resigned
when the cup comes down,
surprised when they're let out
into unexpected air
where at last they are not stymied
by maddening, mystifying glass.
Others are so adept
at swerving from my manoeuvres
they will die within sight
of freedom, or blunder
into a web. The spiders wait.

They never move much
until they sense wings.

Bailing

There must have been a moment
when Noah, 600 years old,
sensing the first drops on his head,
wondered if he'd been too ambitious;
thought about maybe stopping
the whole Ark business,
toyed with the easier option
of going down with the flood.

I picture him, cringing,
as the animals hoof
up the gangplank – snorting, farting
and tossing their horns.
Or, bilious and exhausted,
after 100 days of nothing
but queasy waves, and quarrels
with his stir-crazy family.

Did he baulk at the horizon,
the empty-beaked raven,
trying not to think
of the dwindling supplies?
The leak in the hold
poorly stoppered,
the weakness
in his old hands.
The not knowing
when this test of faith
would be lifted.

Divination

The pipe that ferries
our kitchen waste
is plugged again.
Bending in the rain
over the open shore
I pour hot water,
caustic soda, vinegar;
poke with a stick,
wiggle my snake:
Miss Marple of the drains.
At last I get inspired,
seek the pipe
at its further end,
dig till I find
the square metal lid.
Pulled off it reveals
my culprit: a ball
of pale compacted goo
hard as a rock. How could
our oils of olive and coconut
morph to such a state?
I seize it up,
as if it were a find
of solid gold,
and watch in hallelujah mode
the waters gush,
sluicing the sluggish load
out of sight.

I squat, sodden,
streaked with filth,
my face alight. At least
one block's been cleared.

Sizing Up

Ascending to the menswear store,
I listen to the pigeons on the roof,
their scuffles, bills and croons.

The snug fit of the jacket pleases you;
the trousers' tailored waist. Sleek and natty, unlike
your father's old suit, which is the wrong shape.

You pace towards me, testing your steps
as you once did when you were small.
At seventeen, this new ensemble

lends you a panther's prowling grace,
yet beneath the jacket's sharp lapels
beats a tender heart; above, beams a boy's face.

I hope the world will stretch you lightly,
and not to ripping point, my shining son.
That you'll have your natural span.

That love will come for you
and fold you in her arms,
when I no longer can.

You walk away.
The pigeons fall silent.
I go to pay.

Recess

Driving over the hill
drenched in rain
I find a static line
of traffic;
I slam the brake,
aquaplane straight
into the car in front,
the crunch muting
as the airbags erupt
while I fade to black fuzz,
far from my mangled bonnet,
through which I hear
the voice of my friend, urgent:
Get out of the car!
I shove the door,
suddenly afraid of the smoke,
the burning smell,
crawl through
the blooming, dusty ghosts.
I get out of that car
and I am alive.
It's dead though,
full of the corpsed airbags.
And as the kind men come
to find us
in our disastrous
rainsoaked damage,
with their young faces
full of concern,
I begin to cry.

Dancing Queens

(for Catherine Harris)

Hair lemon-washed,
eyelids spangled blue,
we pretended to be older
for the disco doormen
in the Marine Hotel.

Now we stomp its boards
to celebrate our sixties,
a new decade,
just breached.

We shimmy, gyrate,
shake and spin
our mysterious bodies
that have crawled, sailed,
birthed and mourned,
yet in many ways
feel the same.

We spiral back to lost scenes:
singing along
to your sister's Beatles tunes,
infusing 'Yesterday'
with every tremolo
of our young throats;
sneaking to the kitchen
for spoonfuls of Horlicks powder,
crackers and butter –
our 'midnight feasts';

and later, laughing
in hysterical disbelief

at the book
your mother gave you:
The Facts of Life.

The Seal

What are you doing
in my element?
The seal's black eyes
challenge me
as I flail
in the tall waves,
seaweed tangling my legs.

Wild, whiskered
canine of the salt,
he appraises me
with a hunter's look:
he's far too close,
with a head on him
like a bucket.
I scrabble and squawk
kicking to cheat the tide
and his looming bulk,
to show my friend I'm safe:
Really I am – I can do this!

Just as my feet
find purchase
a wave breaks:
I'm thrown,
tumbled, reefed
as the water
curls and separates,
sand whirling my ears,
weed muddling my hair
shingle scrubbing me raw.

I shove up: shaken,
snot-slimed,
flesh marbled cold.
The seal drifts north,
sinking and surfacing
in comfort.
I stumble
in the stinging spray:
clumsy interloper,
refusing to buckle.

NOTES

Foxed (24

I gave this fox a daily homeopathic remedy, and he responded to the treatment eventually – to the extent that his coat grew back. This remedy is available from the National Fox Welfare Society (UK).

Needle (42)

This healthy cat developed a rare reaction to her annual booster shot called 'injection site sarcoma', a deadly form of cancer.

Home to Vote (45)

Many young Irish people living abroad wanted to come home to vote Yes in the referendum to repeal the 8th Amendment (effectively, to legalise abortion in Ireland). Those who couldn't afford the travel expenses received donations from supporters which enabled them to make the journey. Their votes were crucial in ensuring that abortion became legal in Ireland. Up to that time, Irish girls and women with unwanted pregnancies were forced to travel to the UK to obtain a termination. In 2016, an estimated nine Irish girls and women made the journey every single day.

Portrait of the Mother as a Clay Teapot (00)

Irish College is a rite of passage for 13-15 year-olds in Ireland, particularly Dubliners, to improve their Irish language speaking skills. For three weeks they learn Irish in the *Gaeltacht* – remote parts of Ireland, mostly in the West, where Irish is still spoken as a first language. It is often the first time they have spent such a long time away from home, and parents are not encouraged to visit more than once. A *ceilí* is a night of traditional Irish dancing.

Berkeley (74)

In 2015 a group of Irish students went to spend the summer in Berkeley, California. On 16th June, during a 21st birthday party, a 5th-floor balcony collapsed. Seven students died and six were seriously injured. Later it was discovered that the balcony had dry rot due to negligence.

ACKNOWLEDGEMENTS

Acknowledgements are due to the following journals and anthologies in which some of these poems, or versions of them, were first published: *The Banyan Review; The Bealtaine Anthology; Connotation Press: An Online Artifact; Correspondences: An Anthology to Call for an End to Direct Provision* (2019); *Empty House: Poetry and Prose on the Climate Crisis* (Doire Press, 2021); *The Interpreter's House; The Irish Times; Live Encounters; Metamorphic: 21st Century Poets Respond to Ovid* (Recent Work Press, 2017); *The Music of What Happens: The Purple House Anthology of New Writing* (New Island Books, 2020); *New Hibernia Review; One Hand Clapping; Poetry Ireland Review; Reading the Future: New Writing from Ireland* (Arlen House, 2018); *Southword; Washing Windows? Irish Women Write Poetry* (Arlen House, 2017).

My thanks to the Arts Office of Dún Laoghaire/Rathdown County Council for commissioning 'May Swim, White Rock, 2020', 'Salvage' and 'Marking Time, Dalkey' as part of its Artworks Home Project during the Covid-19 lockdown of 2020.

Poet comrades and literary editors have supported me at various stages with the finishing of these poems – if poems are ever really finished. Thanks to Mary O'Malley, Eiléan Ní Chuilleanáin, Colette Bryce, Jim Rogers, David O'Connor, Irish Stanza, and the members of the Last Friday Club. As ever, my heartfelt gratitude to Neil Astley and the team at Bloodaxe Books.